A GUIDEBOOK TO
Dating, Waiting and Choosing a Mate

NORMAN WRIGHT
MARVIN INMON

HARVEST HOUSE PUBLISHERS
Eugene, Oregon 97402

A GUIDEBOOK TO DATING, WAITING AND CHOOSING A MATE

Copyright © 1978 Harvest House Publishers
Eugene, Oregon 97402
Library of Congress Catalog Card Number: 78-26913
ISBN # 0-89081-150-4

Printed in the United States of America.

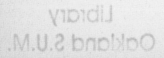

Contents

Chapter 1

To Be or Not to Be—Married

Most people in our society naturally expect that everyone will marry. But observation shows this just isn't so. Most people do marry, but others do not for one reason or another. There are some who, for logical and rational reasons, choose not to marry. For some this decision is made because they simply choose not to marry. For others God has clearly indicated that singleness will be their life-style.

Let's spend some time considering some facts and characteristics about singleness and marriage.

1. Answer the following questions:
   a. What are five healthy reasons for getting married?

   (1) _Emotional fulfillment_

   (2) _Children_

   (3) _Sexual fulfillment_

   (4) _spiritual helpmate_

   (5) _Close friendship_

   b. What are five unhealthy reasons for getting married?

   (1) _Loss of Personal freedom_

(2) Turning your attention from God to family

(3) Extra financial Burden

(4) Inlaw-Family Problems

(5) Child Problems

c. What are five healthy reasons for remaining single?

(1) Personal Freedom

(2) Financial Freedom.

(3) Spiritual Freedom.

(4) Professional Freedom.

(5) Emotional freedom.

d. What are five unhealthy reasons for remaining single?

(1) loneliness

(2) Diet

(3) No help

(4) No children

(5) Companionship
Stigma

2. Describe what you believe are some possible bene-

fits of single life.

Personal, financial, Spiritual freedom

3. What are some possible limitations of married life?

Being burdened with family Cares & Problems .

4. What are some possible benefits of married life?

Companionship, not being lonely, etc.

5. What are some possible limitations of single life?

No Companionship; being lonely.

6. What are some pressures that drive people to marry?

Sex, The stigma of being single, lonelyness

7. At this time in your life are you planning on marriage or singleness as your life-style? What principles or indications have led you to this decision?

Marriage

8. Describe the guidelines or procedures you would use to determine if singleness is for you.

It's not.

Consider what Tim Stafford has said about singleness.

". . . God may want you to be single. He wants everyone to be single for at least a part of life. And the Bible doesn't talk about singleness as second-rate. In fact, it speaks of it positively. In the Middle Ages Christians went too far, and *marriage* was regarded as second-rate. We seem to have swung the other way now, and need to balance in the middle. Both marriage and singleness are gifts from God.

"Ponder for a minute one fact: Jesus Christ, our Lord, never married. He never had sexual intercourse. Yet He was perfect, and perfectly fulfilled. He lived the kind of life we want to imitate. That doesn't mean we ought to all want to be single: there's no doubt marriage is the best way for most men and women. But it should say one thing for certain: singleness need not be second-rate. It need not be unfulfilled. It need not be unhappy. When well-meaning people ask me, 'What's a nice guy like you doing without a wife?' I sometimes answer, with a grin, 'I'm just hoping to be more like Jesus!'

"Paul wasn't married either, at least at the height of his career. He wrote recommending the single life in 1 Corinthians 7, calling it a gift. (Strange that this is the one gift most would prefer to exchange.) And Jesus Himself, in Matthew 19:10-12, talks positively about the reasons some people should remain unmarried.

"Some people, of course, try to peer into the future and find out whether God has given them the gift of singleness. They want to know, I guess, whether someday God is going to award them a spouse, or whether they should forget about relating to the opposite sex, shrug their shoulders, and settle down to the long grind. Maybe God does actually tell some people ahead of time whether they will or won't be married. But most of us seem to find out what He wants one day at a time. I have no reason to believe that a 'gift' of singleness can't be temporary. God may completely fulfill you as a single person at one stage of life, but at another He might call you to marriage. By the same token, a married man, for example, never knows when his spouse's death might call him back to the 'gift' of singleness.

"One of the saddest things I see, then, is the tendency for single people to live life as though waiting for something or someone to happen to them. They act as though they are in limbo, waiting to become capable of life when the magic day at the altar comes. Of course, they're usually disappointed. In some cases they become such poor specimens of humanity that no one wants to marry them. More often they do get married only to discover that they haven't received the key to life: the initiative and character they should have developed before marriage is exactly what they need in marriage. And they are still lonely and frustrated.

"What do you do with a gift? You open it. You admire it. You thank the giver. You use it. And this is what we ought to do with the singleness God has called us to for the present.

"Much has been written about the special opportunities a single person has. There is, as Paul points out in 1 Corinthians 7:32-34, greater freedom to help other people, freedom to spend time with God, freedom to develop himself, freedom to have fun. But this gift, however good, is worth little unless it is put to use. Our culture, especially our Christian culture, has stressed repeatedly that a good marriage takes work. It holds up for admiration those who have formed 'a good marriage.' But I've seldom heard anyone emphasize the fact that a good single life also takes work. I've never heard anyone compliment a person for having created a good single life-style. This creates an atmosphere in which telling single people they have received a gift is rather like convincing a small child that liver ought to taste good, because it's 'good for you.'

"Singleness, as I see it, is not so much a state we've arrived at as an open door, a set of opportunities for us to follow up." [1]

What do you think about his suggestions?

9. What do the following verses say about marriage and singleness?

a. 1 Corinthians 7:7-9

IT is better To be single, but The singleness is not for everyone.

b. 1 Corinthians 7:32-35

The single Christian Cares more about God Than the married Christian.

c. Matthew 6:33; 19:22

We are not To be Taken up With the material Things of This world, but The Spiritual Things of heaven.

How to Determine if Singleness Is for You

1. Recognize that singleness may be for a period of time (for example, until you are thirty) rather than for all of your life.
2. Recognize that it is easier to decide that singleness is not for you and get married than to realize you should have remained single once you are married.
3. Are you able to live with the idea that you might remain single all your life?
4. Is your desire to serve God complicated by the thought of a marriage partner?
5. Are you able to enjoy yourself without feeling the need for a lot of dates?
6. Could you live out the conditions of a vow to God to remain single for a period of time (for example, one year, five years, etc.) without seriously dating?
7. Do you see the advantages of singleness outweighing the advantages of marriage?
8. Do you see God calling you to a form of service that would be difficult if you were married (for example, work in the inner city, work in primitive mission projects)?
9. Are you willing to live with the stigma of being single if this is what God wants?
10. If you think singleness is for you, try it for a specific period of time. (Go for one year without a date, devoting your normal dating time to serving God.) If you fail, there should be no thought of having fallen out of favor with God. This is just an experiment. It is similar to trying to go to the mission field and finding that you can't. You can still serve God effectively wherever you are. However, you should be as open to God's call to single living as you are to any other call He might give you.[2]

Dating Questions for Young Adults

1. What is the purpose of dating?

   Having fun, getting to know someone.

2. What qualities in your life do you have to offer a dating partner?

   Good, Clean fun.

3. What qualities do you want to see in a person you date?

   That They have a good Personality and like To have fun.

4. What would you like to do on your dates and where would you like to go? Are there some types of dating activities that you feel you will not become involved in?

   Bowling, football, baseball games, movies, dinner.

5. Do you want to date Christians or non-Christians? Why?

Christian - moral Values.

6. How late should you be allowed to stay out on dates? Does it depend on the activity? Explain.

My mother said 12:00!

7. How often should you be allowed to date each week?

Once a week.

8. At what age should you be allowed to date? Why did you choose that age?

My mother said the magic number was 16 - not too bad.

9. How do you feel about your parents meeting the person you date before you go out with him or her?

They should if at all possible.

10. At what age do you want to become engaged? Marry?

21.

11. How can you determine God's will for the person you marry? What scriptural principles would help you?

To love / serve God
Matt. 22:37-40

12. How do you think your parents would answer each of these questions?

Close To mine.

References

1. Tim Stafford, *A Love Story* (Grand Rapids: Zondervan, 1977), pp. 91-93.

2. Adapted from Charles Cerling, "Is Marriage for You? A High School Curriculum," *Marriage & Family Resource Newsletter*, Vol. 3, No. 6 (June/July 1977).

NOTES

NOTES

_____

_____

_____

_____

_____

_____

_____

_____

_____

_____

_____

_____

Chapter 2
Are You the One?

Dating, courtship, and marriage are all part of the great American dream. But what is involved in each of these three activities? That's what this workbook is all about. But first, let's find out what you believe.

1. Define marriage. Give as detailed a description of marriage as you possibly can.

   Two People becoming one.

2. Do you believe that marriage is a contract? Why or why not?

   No - it is a way of life.

Marriage contains a unique and interesting potential. As one optimist put it, "Marriage is the only game of chance in town where both players can either win or both lose!" We hope that if you choose to marry your marriage will be rewarding and fulfilling. Consider then what others have said about marriage. Circle the portions of these quotes that you agree with.

"Marriage resembles a pair of shears, so joined that they cannot be separated; often moving in opposite directions, yet always punishing anyone who comes between them."[1]

"Is marriage a private action of two persons in love,

or a public act of pledging a contract? Neither, it is something other. Very much other! Basically, the Christain view of marriage is not that it is primarily or essentially a binding legal or social contract. The Christian understands marriage as a covenant made under God and in the presence of fellow members of the Christian family. Such a pledge endures, not because of the force of law or the fear of its sanctions, but because an unconditional covenant has been made. A covenant more solemn, more binding, more permanent than any legal contract." [2]

"Marriage does not demand perfection. But it must be given priority. It is an institution for sinners. No one else need apply. But it finds its finest glory when sinners see it as God's way of leading us through His ultimate curriculum of love and righteousness." [3]

". . . Marriage is a relationship between man and woman intended by God to be a monogamous relationship, intended to be a permanent bond in which many needs are satisfied—the need to love and be loved, the need for deep friendship, for sharing, for companionship, for sexual satisfaction, for children, the need to escape loneliness. Marriage ought to be a bond of love, reflecting the love Christ has for His people, a bond of sacrificial love where husband and wife have become one, one flesh, a unity." [4]

1. According to Genesis 2:18-25, who originated the marriage institution?

2. What are the purposes of marriage and why was it originated? (See Gen. 1:28; 2:18; Eph. 5:22-32.)

   (1) _____

(2) _____

(3) _____

(4) _____

Read Matthew 7:24-27. This passage is talking about building your house upon a firm foundation. List what you believe are ten firm foundation stones which will go into making a solid marriage relationship.

1. _____

2. _____

3. _____

4. _____

5 _____

6. _____

7. _____

8. _____

9. _____

10. _____

Reasons for Marriage

There are many reasons and motivating factors for marriage. What are yours? Have you ever thought about them? Here are two very important questions for you to answer and then discuss with your fiance, if you are engaged, or with a parent or friend.

1. What will you receive from marriage that you would not receive by remaining single?

2. Describe the type of marriage you want if you marry. Give as much description as you can.

3. List in detail the ten most important characteristics or qualities that you want in the person you someday marry.

    (1) _____

    (2) _____

    (3) _____

    (4) _____

    (5) _____

    (6) _____

    (7) _____

    (8) _____

    (9) _____

    (10) _____

Dating Questions for Parents

Ask your parents to answer these questions.

1. What qualities does your son or daughter have to offer a person he or she might date?

2. In which area do you trust your son or daughter most?

3. In which area do you have some concerns and how do you plan to assist your son or daughter in strengthening this area?

4. What is the purpose of dating?

5. What qualities would you like to see in the person your son or daughter dates?

6. Should your son or daughter date just Christians or both Christians and non-Christians?

7. What dating activities are permissible and which ones would you not want him to become involved with?

8. What time do you feel your son or daughter needs to return home after a date? Does it depend upon the activity? If so, explain.

9. How often can your son or daughter date each week?

10. At what age will your son or daughter be able to date? Will these be single dates or dates in a group?

11. If you have a daughter, will you ask to meet the boy before she dates him? If so, what would you discuss? What would you ask him?

12. Will you encourage your son or daughter to bring his date to dinner or to visit or have parties at your home? Why?

13. At what age do you feel comfortable about your son or daughter becoming engaged or marrying? Should he or she finish vocational training or college first?

14. Go back over all these questions and attempt to answer them as you think your son or daughter will answer them. You may need some time to discuss these questions with your spouse.

References

1. Sydney Smith, *Lady Holland's Memoir*, Vol. I (Longman, Brown, Green & Longman, 1855).

2. David Augsburger, *Cherishable: Love and Marriage* (Scottsdate, Pa.: Herald Press, 1971), p. 16.

3. From a message by Dr. David Hubbard, President of Fuller Theological Seminary.

4. Daniel Freeman, "Why Get Married?" *Theology News and Notes of Fuller Theological Seminary*, XIX, 4 (December 1973), 17.

NOTES

Yoked - Webster -

Marrage is a mortal example of the
commitment between Christ & His
Church.

NOTES

NOTES

Chapter 3

My Family, Your Family, Our Family

1. Complete the following family evaluation.
   a. If you were to describe or define your own family in one word, what would the word be?

   b. What strengths do you see in your own family?

   c. What strengths do you see in your parents? Have you ever told them that you are aware of these strengths and appreciate them?

   d. Write down the goals you have for your family life.

   e. What do you think parents or other teenagers would say about your family?

   f. What do your parents do that makes you feel loved or of value?

g. What do you do that expresses your love toward your family?

h. What expectations does God have for your family?

i. What do you feel is a weak area in your family life?

j. What can you do to strengthen this weak area, and what can you do to reach the goals that you have for your family life?

If you are seriously dating someone at the present time, go back over these questions once again and answer them as you see your partner's family.

2. Let's consider your family once again. What are the characteristics of your family? First, draw a picture of your family. Don't be concerned about your artistic ability. Just draw all of the family members the best way you can.

Now that you've drawn your family, what do you
see? Why did you place family members where they
are? Ask a friend what he or she sees in your family
description.

3. Now list all of the characteristics of your family
that you can think of.

4. Describe in detail how you would like your parents
to behave or respond to:
a. Your dating partner

b. Your spouse when married

5. Describe in detail how you would like your dating
partner's parents to behave or respond to you.

Family Characteristics

6. Read over the following Family Rating Scale. Look at the two words that are opposite on each line. First, rate yourself on the 1-to-10 scale by circling the number that you think best describes yourself. Then place a P beside the number that best describes your partner, if you are dating or engaged. Place your own initials on the line where you think your parents would place you. Place a D on the scale at the point that you think best describes your dad, and an M on the scale at the point that you think your partner or friends would place you. When you have completed this, consider what you can do at this point in your life to bring about changes in the areas in which you feel changes should be made.

Family Rating Scale

Perfectionistic								Could not care less	
1	2	3	4	5	6	7	8	9	10

Rejecting									Accepting
1	2	3	4	5	6	7	8	9	10

Overprotective							Underprotective		
1	2	3	4	5	6	7	8	9	10

Overindulgent								Stingy	
1	2	3	4	5	6	7	8	9	10

Overpermissive								Legalistic	
1	2	3	4	5	6	7	8	9	10

Severe								Trustworthy	
1	2	3	4	5	6	7	8	9	10

Inconsistent								Consistent	
1	2	3	4	5	6	7	8	9	10

Faulty model								Godly model	
1	2	3	4	5	6	7	8	9	10

Double binding								Enabling	
1	2	3	4	5	6	7	8	9	10

Here are some vital questions to consider and answer if you are planning on marriage. One of the reasons for the emphasis upon you and your present family is that the way you respond to and interact with your parents will have an effect upon your own marriage and in-law relationships.

1. What have you done in the past to let your parents know that they are important to you? If you are engaged, what have you done in the past to let your fiance's parents know that they are important to you?
2. During the past two weeks, what have you done to express your positive feelings toward these people?
3. What new things could you say or do that would let them know they are important to you?
4. Describe what you have done to discover, from your parents and your fiancé's parents, (if you are engaged) what kind of relationship they expect from you? What can you do about this in the future?
5. In the past how have you helped your parents or your fiancé's parents meet their own needs and develop a greater meaning in life? How can you help them in the future?
6. If they have had difficulty in communicating with you in the past, how did you respond to them? How can you be more helpful in the future?
7. In the past what have you done with your parents or future in-laws to make it easier for them to demonstrate love toward you? How can you improve this in the future?
8. What have you done in the past to assist your parents or future in-laws to receive love from you? What have you done to demonstrate love to them?

NOTES

NOTES

NOTES

Chapter 4

Expectations

"A Little Serious Conversation, Please!"

In this activity you will have the opportunity to settle down with one or both of your parents in a serious discussion about their dating habits and their expectations for your dating behavior. Do you think that dating has really changed since the time your parents were your age? Or have only the activities changed?

Choose a time when you can spend a couple of hours with the parent you are interviewing and feel free to expand on any of the questions in this chapter. We encourage you to ask questions of your own and be willing to share openly your feelings about the same questions with the parent or parents being interviewed. You might also wish to use the same set of questions with another adult, a friend of your own age, or the person you are dating.

You will be asked to share some of your thoughts with others if you are using this workbook in a classroom situation.

1. What is the purpose of dating? Getting to know people of the opposite sex. Having Fun

2. What was your first date like? Scary! A double date with my sister

3. Most parents expect certain things from their children in terms of their dating behavior. What expectations did your parents have for your dating

activity? List ten expectations placed upon you by your parents.

(1) _Date ony good girls._

(2) _Don't get serious._

(3) _Stay pure. No sex._

(4) _____

(5) _____

(6) _____

(7) _____

(8) _____

(9) _____

(10) _____

4. Now that you are a parent what do you expect from your children in a dating relationship? List ten expectations you have for your son or daughters dating behavior.

(1) _____

(2) _____

(3) _____

(4) _____

(5) _____

(6) _____

(7) _____

(8) _____

(9) _____

(10)_____

5. Since you have certain expectations for my behavior, you must expect certain things from the persons I date. What do you expect from them concerning the way they relate to you?

What expectations do you have for them concerning their behavior and treatment of me?

6. What kind of person should I date? What should their qualifications be, their background, and their education?

7. How would you feel if I failed to meet your expectations?

What feelings would you experience if my date failed to meet your expectations?

8. When you were dating what did you expect from a date and from the person you were dating?

9. How would you describe my ideal dating partner? Give eight characteristics.

(1) _____

(2) _____

(3) _____

(4) _____

(5) _____

(6) _____

(7) _____

(8) _____

10. What is the purpose of an engagement?

How will I know when I am ready to become engaged?

How is an engagement different from dating?

11. What kind of a person are you looking for me to marry?

What are ten positive characteristics I have to offer a marriage partner?

(1) _____

(2) _____

(3) _____

(4) _____

(5) _____

(6) _____

(7) _____

(8) _____

(9) _____

(10) _____

What are five negative characteristics I have which may hinder building a positive marital relationship?

(1) _____

(2) _____

(3) _____

(4) _____

(5) _____

12. What were the three major problems you encountered during your first year of marriage, and how did you work them out?

(1) _____

(2) _____

(3) _____

13. What happened the first time one of your expectations was not met by your partner?

How do you resolve conflict in your relationship?

Although I see interaction between my parents, sometimes appearances are not all they are cracked up to be. How are decisions made in our home, and who has the last word in them?

14. If you did not approve of my choice for either a date or a marriage partner, how would you feel? What would you say or do, positively or negatively, in that situation?

"A Little Serious Consideration, Please!"

Now that you have had the opportunity to discuss with your parents their expectations and feelings about your dating and marriage behavior (and for those of you who are using this workbook in the classroom and have had the opportunity to discuss with other couples and your peers their expectations for dating and marriage), take a few minutes to write out your own expectations.

1. Dating: What do you expect from yourself, as a date?

What do you expect from your dating partners?

2. Engagement: What do you expect from engagement? What will you contribute to your engagement?

3. Marriage: What are your expectations for your marriage? What are your expectations for a marital partner? How would you feel if he or she failed to meet all of your expectations?

NOTES

_____

_____

_____

_____

_____

_____

_____

_____

_____

_____

_____

_____

_____

_____

_____

_____

_____

NOTES

Chapter 5

Self-Esteem and Marriage

The question "What am I?" usually points to the marks of identification that distinguish us from other people and make us unique. We give name, sex, age, height, weight (although some of us don't like to give our weight), nationality, etc., in response to this question.

"What am I?" is usually a label. I am a high school student, football player, cheerleader, straight-A student, or straight-D student.

"Why am I?" is a question pointing to our reason for living and existence.

Our self-concept is usually built upon the way we have been answering these questions. It is our sense of being somebody.

Now let's take this process of analyzing our self-concept a step further. Complete the statement "I am . . ." ten times. Each sentence should refer to yourself.

1. I am _____

2. I am _____

3. I am _____

4. I am _____

5. I am _____

6. I am _____

7. I am _____

8. I am _____

9. I am _____

10. I am _____

Now go back and evaluate.
1. Put a P by each positive statement and an N by each negative one.
2. Put an FM beside each statement that is true because another family member has said so.
3. Put an F beside each statement that is true because your friends have said so.
4. Put a G beside each statement that is true because God says so.
5. Put a U beside each statement that is unconfirmed by anybody.

Your Identity

Your identity or self-image is crucial. It affects your relationship with God, with your family, with your dates, how you perform in school or at work, and the choice of a marriage partner. It can also determine what you receive from life.

Your self-image has a controlling influence on your mind. A person's opinion of himself affects his interpretation of life. A person who thinks unrealistically about himself does so because his self-concept is malformed. If it is severely malformed, he will reject even positive information and responses about himself which others seek to give him.

Have you ever met a person like this? How did he or she behave?

The individual who has a good self-image feels good about himself and likes himself. He accepts both his positive qualities and his weaknesses. He is confident but he is also realistic. He can handle other people's reactions, both positive and negative. He sets out to accomplish what he is capable of doing and feels that others will respond to him. He has confidence in his perceptions, ability, and judgments. He is not afraid to become involved in the lives of other people nor to allow others to become involved in his life. And he is not defensive.

But the person who has a poor self-image is just the opposite. He doesn't trust himself, and is usually apprehensive about expressing his ideas for fear of attracting the attention of others. He may withdraw and live in the shadow of others or his social group. He is overly aware of himself and often has a morbid preoccupation with his problems.

Because he is so preoccupied with himself, he does not correctly see the attitudes others have toward him. He believes that other people must feel the same about him as he feels about himself. Since he feels other people do not want to include him in their group, he is hesitant to join them for fear of rejection. He can mingle with people but is hesitant to become honestly and openly involved with them. His avoidance of others has the effect of reinforcing his low self-image.

How will your self-concept affect your dating life and the selection of a marriage partner?

Consider these questions:

1. How do you treat yourself?

2. Have you ever thought of yourself as being a parent to yourself?

3. What kind of a parent are you?

4. Do you treat yourself with scorn and disrespect?

5. Do you punish yourself?

6. Do you expect and demand too much of yourself?

7. Does the way you treat yourself reflect upon your concept of God?

8. Does God treat you in the same manner that you treat yourself?

9. What do these scriptures say about how we should view ourselves? Read the following passages and write your responses here.

   Psalm 139:14-16

   Ephesians 2:10

   Philippians 1:6

1 Peter 2:9

1 Corinthians 4:2-5

2 Corinthians 12:9

A Model for Building Self-Esteem

1. What do you think people do or use to build their self-concept?

2. What do you use?

3. What are some good foundations to use to build self-esteem and some that are not solid enough?

Basis for a Healthy Self-Concept

Dr. Maurice Wagner, in his excellent book *The Sensation of Being Somebody*, suggested that our self-concept (our identity) is built upon two foundations. One is called the functional foundation and the other is called the feeling foundation.[1]

The functional foundation has three parts. The aspect of *appearance* underlies much of our thinking and our conversation. The question you ask here is, How do I look? How we view our bodies, our dress, and our personal grooming is part of our appearance. Take a minute now and write down how you feel about how you look.

Now write down how you would feel about yourself if the positive appearance that you have were taken away.

The aspect of *performance* contains the question, How am I doing? This is how we view our abilities, skills, knowledge, and sense of responsibility. Write down what you are good at. It might be some task or activity that only you are aware of, or, perhaps many people might know about it.

Now write down how you would feel about yourself if you were no longer able to perform as you once did.

The third area is that of *status*. The question here is, How important am I? We all want to feel admired and respected. Status can come from our family name, education, position, job, groups of friends we associate with, the person we are dating, places we go, car we ride in, if we are engaged, etc. The three parts of the functional foundation of self-image come about from how we feel treated by other people. When we are thinking of our appearance, performance, or status, it is as if we imagine that we are standing off and looking at ourselves from the outside.

What do you do to give yourself status? What makes you feel important?

How would you feel if this were taken from you? Would you still feel good about yourself? Would you still like yourself?

Which of these areas do you feel are most important in your own life? Is your self-concept based mostly on status, performance, or appearance?

The second foundation of self-concept suggested by Dr. Wagner is feelings. He noted three kinds of feelings that have unusual significance in forming the essential elements of self-concept: belongingness, worthiness, and competence. These three feelings constitute the mental structure of the self-concept like the three legs of a tripod support its top. If any one of the three begins to weaken, the self-concept totters.

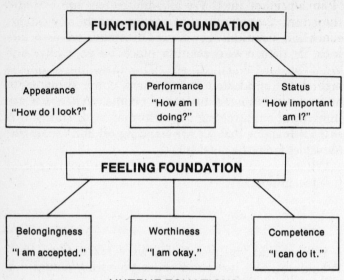

SELF-CONCEPT

FUNCTIONAL FOUNDATION

Appearance	Performance	Status
"How do I look?"	"How am I doing?"	"How important am I?"

FEELING FOUNDATION

Belongingness	Worthiness	Competence
"I am accepted."	"I am okay."	"I can do it."

UNTRUE EQUATIONS

Appearance + Admiration = Whole Person
Performance + Accomplishments = Whole Person
Status + Recognition = Whole Person

THE CORRECT EQUATION

God + You = Whole Person

Belongingness is the awareness of being wanted, accepted, cared for, and enjoyed. Are you aware of being wanted? By whom? Are you accepted? By whom? How do you know? Do others enjoy you? Do you enjoy yourself? How do you know?

Worthiness is a feeling of "I am good," "I count," and "I am all right." People feel worthy when they do what they think they should. The feeling is verified when we sense that others have positive attitudes toward us. We look for their endorsement of our actions. A feeling of worthiness is related to a sense of being right and doing right in our eyes and in the eyes of others. Belongingness and worthiness are similar. A person feels good about himself when accepted by others. When do you feel most worthy? What do you have to feel worthy about? Who else sees you as worthy?

Competence is a feeling of adequacy. It is the feeling "I can," "I have the ability or strength to do it." A feeling of adequacy is built upon present as well as past accomplishments. It is based upon the achievement of goals and ideals that we have for ourself. When do you feel most adequate? Who else sees you as adequate?

Many of us build our self-image or identity primarily upon what we think others think or feel about us. Is this valid? Can we always trust our perceptions of how others perceive us, or is there a better way?

Many of us have built our identity over the years by getting an impression about ourselves from our parents or friends. We have also gone about confirming this impression. If enough people reaffirm what we think about ourselves, this thought or belief becomes part of our self-identity. The problem that exists here is that sometimes people agree with us just to be nice or because they don't care about us enough to confront us with the truth. Thus we get distorted information, build distorted self-images, and feel insecure about ourselves. Some of us have lived in home atmospheres where we have received untrue information about ourselves because of problems existing in other persons. When we live with others who are overly critical and negative and constantly putting us down, we may come to believe that we are "no good." This is the problem of basing our self-concept solely upon what other people say, think, or feel.

Many of us have developed equations by which we seek to become somebody. Going back to the functional foundation of our self-concept, we have developed the equation of Appearance + Admiration = Whole Person. But this does not balance because we are not the sum total of how we appear or what others admiringly think of us. Dress and looks are somewhat important but not to the extent that some of us have made them. Many teenagers and adults spend hours working on their looks and style in order to draw attention to themselves. Often they ask others how they look over and over again. When they receive compliments, however, they are not always satisfied, for if they were, why would they keep working and working on their appearance?

Another question we have developed is Performance + Accomplishment = Whole Person. But we are more than the sum total of our skills and the recognized abilities we have developed. Sometimes parents do not give love and acceptance unless the child or teenager achieves. Even then some parents may not give recognition because, as one parent said, "I don't want him to become lazy and slack off. If I tell him that he did a good job, he'll get lazy." Sometimes a person feels he must perform for his marriage partner so that he will not be rejected.

Men use performance as a standard more than women do. High school boys build much of their self-concept, for example, upon how well they do in sports. Or if not in that, in music, grades, goofing off, etc. Many men build their self-concept upon how well they do in their job. Their job actually becomes an extension of themselves. They throw themselves into it and spend many hours trying to achieve. But if their job fails, so go their feelings of worth.

A third equation is Status + Recognition = Whole Person. This equation is also untrue, for we are more than anyone thinks of us.

Try as we might by our appearance, performance, or social status to find ways to build a sense of being somebody, we always come short of satisfaction.

We have been loved unconditionally and voluntarily by God, and He has manifested that love at Calvary. When we stop trying to qualify for His love and simply accept Him as our Savior we enter into a new set of values, a new dimension of self-identity. We find a new equation for our sense of being somebody, and this one truly balances. It is God + Me = Whole Person.[2]

(If you are interested in learning more about building your self-concept see *Improving Your Self-Image* by H. Norman Wright. This is available in both book and cassette form and is published by Harvest House Publishers.)

References

1. Maurice Wagner, *The Sensation of Being Somebody* (Grand Rapids: Zondervan, 1975), p. 37.

2. Ibid., p. 162, 163.

NOTES

NOTES

NOTES

Chapter 6

I Need, You Need: To Meet a Need

Need Assessment Worksheet

Every person has needs. You have some and so does your dating partner. Below are listed several needs which most of us experience at one point in time or another. It is important that we understand our level of need and the areas of need that we are capable of meeting in the lives of others. Unfulfilled needs in the dating or marital relationships have a tendency either to cloud or to confuse the growth of the relationship. If we have an unfulfilled need for security in any relationship we enter into, it is possible that we may respond to our partner with distrust, communication may break down, we may fail to recognize the value of something, or our sense of self-esteem may be shattered.

It is important not only that we understand our need level and our ability to meet specific needs, but also that we consider possible outcomes of unfulfilled needs in our dating or marital relationships.

The Need Assessment Worksheet is designed to, *first* evaluate your level of need on a continuum of one to ten. (Write your first name at your level of need, with zero being "not a need in my life currently" and ten being "a need which must be met at this point in time by another.") *Second*, it is to serve as a measure of your ability to meet this need in the life of another individual whether through dating or marriage. Place your initials at the point that represents your ability to meet that need in another individual. *Third*, it helps you to establish specific and measurable ways in which each need can be met in your life (by filling in the space provided). *Fourth*, it will assist you to establish specific and measurable ways in which you can meet each need in another individual (by filling in the space provided). *Last*, this project will help you consider what a marriage would be like if that specific need were not fulfilled and the possible problems and responses you could encounter in your marriage.

1. My level of need (insert your first name)_____
   My ability to meet this need in another (insert your initials)_____.
   If you have a steady date or are engaged, do the same as above, inserting the first name of your partner at his level of need and his initials at his ability to meet that need in you.
2. After assessing the above, fill in the spaces provided for each of the following questions:
   a. This need can be met best in me by:
   b. I have the ability to meet this need by:
   c. If this need were not met in a marital relationship, some possible outcomes or problems may be:

Security

0	1	2	3	4	5	6	7	8	9	10

This need can best be met in me by:

I have the ability to meet this need by:

If this need were not met, some possible outcomes or problems may be:

Respect

0	1	2	3	4	5	6	7	8	9	10

This need can best be met in me by :

I have the ability to meet this need by :

If this need were not met, some possible outcomes or problems may be :

Communication

0	1	2	3	4	5	6	7	8	9	10

This need can best be met in me by :

I have the ability to meet this need by :

If this need were not met, some possible outcomes or problems may be :

Care

0	1	2	3	4	5	6	7	8	9	10

This need can best be met in me by :

I have the ability to meet this need by :

If this need were not met, some possible outcomes or problems may be :

Autonomy/Independence

0	1	2	3	4	5	6	7	8	9	10

This need can best be met in me by :

I have the ability to meet this need by :

If this need were not met, some possible outcomes or problems may be :

Attention

0	1	2	3	4	5	6	7	8	9	10

This need can best be met in me by :

I have the ability to meet this need by :

If this need were not met, some possible outcomes or problems may be :

Companionship

0	1	2	3	4	5	6	7	8	9	10

This need can best be met in me by :

I have the ability to meet this need by :

If this need were not met, some possible outcomes or problems may be :

Understanding

0	1	2	3	4	5	6	7	8	9	10

This need can best be met in me by :

I have the ability to meet this need by :

If this need were not met, some possible outcomes or problems may be :

Acceptance

0   1   2   3   4   5   6   7   8   9   10

This need can best be met in me by:

I have the ability to meet this need by:

If this need were not met, some possible outcomes or problems may be:

Trust

0   1   2   3   4   5   6   7   8   9   10

This need can best be met in me by:

I have the ability to meet this need by:

If this need were not met, some possible outcomes or problems may be:

Achievement

0   1   2   3   4   5   6   7   8   9   10

This need can best be met in me by:

I have the ability to meet this need by:

If this need were not met, some possible outcomes or problems may be:

Self-Worth/Self-Esteem

0   1   2   3   4   5   6   7   8   9   10

This need can best be met in me by:

I have the ability to meet this need by:

If this need were not met, some possible outcomes or problems may be:

Love

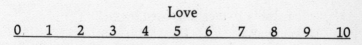

0   1   2   3   4   5   6   7   8   9   10

This need can best be met in me by:

I have the ability to meet this need by:

If this need were not met, some possible outcomes or problems may be :

Stability

0	1	2	3	4	5	6	7	8	9	10

This need can best be met in me by:

I have the ability to meet this need by :

If this need were not met, some possible outcomes or problems may be :

Freedom To Be Me

0	1	2	3	4	5	6	7	8	9	10

This need can best be met in me by :

I have the ability to meet this need by :

If this need were not met, some possible outcomes or problems may be :

To Meet Another's Needs

0	1	2	3	4	5	6	7	8	9	10

This need can best be met in me by :

I have the ability to meet this need by :

If this need were not met, some possible outcomes or problems may be :

Others which you may wish to consider include :

Physical needs	Commitment	A sense of humor
Deference—the ability to admire or praise	Sympathy To feel good Share	To be heard Someone I can depend on
Purpose	Success	

Parental Need Assessment Worksheet

After you have completed the Need Assessment Worksheet, ask one or both of your parents to complete the parental need assessment for you by:

1. Placing their son or daughter's first name at his level of need.
2. Placing their son or daughter's initial at his ability to meet his need.
3. Answering the following questions in the spaces provided following the need assessment continuum:
   a. I have attempted to meet this need in my son or daughter by:
   b. My son or daughter's future spouse can meet this need by:
   c. This need could present the following problems for my son or daughter in his marriage:

Security

0   1   2   3   4   5   6   7   8   9   10

I have attempted to meet this need in my son or daughter by :

My son or daughter's future spouse can meet this need by :

This need could present the following problems for my son or daughter in his marriage :

Respect

0   1   2   3   4   5   6   7   8   9   10

I have attempted to meet this need in my son or daughter by :

My son or daughter's future spouse can meet this need by :

This need could present the following problems for my son or daughter in his marriage :

Communication

<u>0   1   2   3   4   5   6   7   8   9   10</u>

I have attempted to meet this need in my son or daughter by :

My son or daughter's future spouse can meet this need by :

This need could present the following problems for my son or daughter in his marriage :

Care

<u>0   1   2   3   4   5   6   7   8   9   10</u>

I have attempted to meet this need in my son or daughter by :

My son or daughter's future spouse can meet this need by :

This need could present the following problems for my son or daughter in his marriage :

Autonomy/Independence

| 0 | 1 | 2 | 3 | 4 | 5 | 6 | 7 | 8 | 9 | 10 |

I have attempted to meet this need in my son or daughter by :

My son or daughter's future spouse can meet this need by :

This need could present the following problems for my son or daughter in his marriage :

Attention

| 0 | 1 | 2 | 3 | 4 | 5 | 6 | 7 | 8 | 9 | 10 |

I have attempted to meet this need in my son or daughter by :

My son or daughter's future spouse can meet this need by :

This need could present the following problems for my son or daughter in his marriage :

Companionship

0	1	2	3	4	5	6	7	8	9	10

I have attempted to meet this need in my son or daughter by :

My son or daughter's future spouse can meet this need by :

This need could present the following problems for my son or daughter in his marriage :

Understanding

0	1	2	3	4	5	6	7	8	9	10

I have attempted to meet this need in my son or daughter by :

My son or daughter's future spouse can meet this need by :

This need could present the following problems for my son or daughter in his marriage :

Acceptance

0	1	2	3	4	5	6	7	8	9	10

I have attempted to meet this need in my son or daughter by :

My son or daughter's future spouse can meet this need by :

This need could present the following problems for my son or daughter in his marriage :

Trust

0	1	2	3	4	5	6	7	8	9	10

I have attempted to meet this need in my son or daughter by :

My son or daughter's future spouse can meet this need by :

This need could present the following problems for my son or daughter in his marriage :

Achievement

0	1	2	3	4	5	6	7	8	9	10

I have attempted to meet this need in my son or daughter by :

My son or daughter's future spouse can meet this need by :

This need could present the following problems for my son or daughter in his marriage :

Self-Worth/Self-Esteem

0	1	2	3	4	5	6	7	8	9	10

I have attempted to meet this need in my son or daughter by :

My son or daughter's future spouse can meet this need by :

This need could present the following problems for my son or daughter in his marriage :

Love

0	1	2	3	4	5	6	7	8	9	10

I have attempted to meet this need in my son or daughter by :

My son or daughter's future spouse can meet this need by :

This need could present the following problems for my son or daughter in his marriage :

Stability

0	1	2	3	4	5	6	7	8	9	10

I have attempted to meet this need in my son or daughter by :

My son or daughter's future spouse can meet this need by :

This need could present the following problems for my son or daughter in his marriage :

Freedom To Be Me

0	1	2	3	4	5	6	7	8	9	10

I have attempted to meet this need in my son or daughter by :

My son or daughter's future spouse can meet this need by :

This need could present the following problems for my son or daughter in his marriage :

To Meet Another's Needs

0	1	2	3	4	5	6	7	8	9	10

I have attempted to meet this need in my son or daughter by :

My son or daughter's future spouse can meet this need by :

This need could present the following problems for my son or daughter in his marriage :

NOTES

NOTES

NOTES

Chapter 7

Intimacy

Intimacy is an aspect of love. It is more than just sex. Because we often confuse intimacy with sex, the church, and parents, often fail to stress the importance of developing truly intimate, but nonsexual relationships with others. As an aspect of love, intimacy should characterize relationships between men, between women, and between men and women.

Intimacy is reached through a progression of steps in a relationship. At first meeting, we are strangers, knowing nothing of each others needs, expectations or motivations. We do not even know whether this encounter will move beyond the level of "strangers." If the relationship continues, we become acquaintances, beginning to share some mutuality. As the relationship continues, perhaps we become friends or close friends. As the relationship develops, we learn to love the other person, to love him or her deeply, and finally we become intimate.

Intimacy can be defined as a developing process over a period of time, which brings individuals into close association, contact, and familiarity—elements necessary for developing warm, long-term relationships. An intimate relationship can be characterized as one in which trust and honesty are evident in all dealings and in which individuals can share their deepest nature (feelings, thoughts, and fears) without fear of undue criticism.

Describe a time when you really felt close to another person:

Describe a time when you felt like a stranger with someone you knew well:

Strangers are not allowed into the Kingdom. Those whom the Father does not know, are not a part of His Body. Turn in your Bible to Ephesians, chapter 5, and look at the path a stranger can lead us down, and what happens as a relationship develops into one of intimacy.

Read Ephesians 5:1-2. What are the characteristics of intimacy involved in having a relationship with God?

In your own words, what does being "imitators of God" mean?

Have you ever been willing to sacrifice your own life for another person? When? Can you think of someone, besides Jesus, who has?

You never know what a stranger is going to be like, until you get to know him. It is possible a stranger may have deceit in his heart, and may attempt to dissuade you from the path of righteousness.

Read Ephesians 5:3-6, and list below some of the potential problems which those who are strangers to the Kingdom may be involved with.

Are people like these, ones which you would choose as friends?

Have you ever been surprised by what a person is really like after you got to know him? How did you end the relationship? Or did they change?

The process of growing up is not always easy, nor are we alone in it; often our friends struggle through it with us and support us. Have you ever done something with your friends, which might be questionable in the sight of others. Maybe your parents raided the watermelon patch in the neighbor's farm, or knocked over outhouses at Halloween. Maybe dad was involved in goldfish eating, or a "panty raid" during his college days. Adolescents struggle with the search for identity, their place in the adult world, and what is right or wrong behavior. We struggle with what is pleasing, what is darkness and light, and it is usually our friends who help us through the process.

Read Ephesians 5:6-14. How does Paul describe this struggle?

What activities have you been involved with, with your friends, that you are proud of?

Have you ever partaken of activities which you would describe as being in darkness? Were they enjoyable? Was there a cost involved which was too high to pay again?

Close friends are those which will usually last for many years. Describe your closest friends in the space below.

Reading Ephesians 5:15-21, what are the positive characteristics of close friends which could be applied to your relationship?

The picture of the marital relationship in Ephesians

5:22-33, paints the ultimate picture of intimacy. It is one of deep love, willingness to sacrifice, investing in the purity of the partner.

List the characteristics painted in this section of Scripture, as belonging to an intimate relationship.

What does submission mean?

What is the meaning of Ephesians 5:21, then?

Is the wife's submission earned by her husband? How?

How does the husband sanctify his wife? Can you list ten ways a man presents his wife without spot or wrinkle, and keeps her holy?

1. _____

2. _____

3. _____

4. _____

5. _____

6. _____

7. _____

8. _____

9. _____

10. _____

Write a paragraph describing the intimacy involved in husbands loving "their own wives as their own bodies." If a marriage was predicated on the development of intimacy to the point of sacrifice, what would it be like?

What would a marriage be like if there were no intimacy except "sex" in the relationship?

NOTES

NOTES

Chapter 8

Becoming a Responsible Adult

Furnishing the Home
("The Buck Stops Here")

In this activity you will have the opportunity to explore the cost and potential problems of furnishing a "first apartment." The first step involved is choosing and pricing specific items of furniture for a two-bedroom apartment. The cost varies from locale to locale. In order to give a realistic figure for your area, it is suggested that you go on a shopping spree to pick out an apartment and the furniture that you would like to have in your first apartment.

Below you will find a list of items which you will need to price, either through window shopping at your local retailer's or through the advertisements in your local newspapers. Remember, this list is not complete and includes only major items of purchase. You may wish to have a single bedroom apartment or maybe rent or purchase a home. Your local real estate agent can give you facts and information on which to base those decisions.

You will need to supply a description and price for each item of furniture listed below. If you are engaged, ask your fiancé to pick his own items and prices. Then compare the two lists and use the difference as a basis for resolving the distinctions between your tastes.

Living Room

Item	Description (What kind or style?	Price
Couch	_____	_____
Chair	_____	_____
Chair	_____	_____
Tables	_____	_____
Lamps (2)	_____	_____
Television	_____	_____

Dining Area

Table	_____	_____
Chairs (4)	_____	_____
_____	_____	_____

Bedroom

Bed	_____	_____
Night Stands	_____	_____
Dresser	_____	_____
Lamps	_____	_____
_____	_____	_____
_____	_____	_____

Bedroom #2

You will have to decide how this bedroom is to be used—as a second bedroom, as a den, or as a study. There are several blank spaces which you can use.

_____	_____	_____
_____	_____	_____
_____	_____	_____
_____	_____	_____

Kitchen

Refrigerator	_____	_____
Stove	_____	_____

Here are some other items which you will need to set up housekeeping and some ideas of things that you might like to have to make living more comfortable.

Stereo	Second bed
Book cases	Corner group set
Piano	Desk
Pictures	Sewing machine
Hutch	Chest of drawers

For the kitchen you might include:

Dishes	Toaster
Pots and pans	Can opener
Bakeware	Iron
Silverware	Electric skillet
Glass/crystal	Blender
Cooking utensils	

You should also consider:

Linens	Towels/wash cloths
Sheets	Pillowcases

On the basis of your shopping spree, how much money would you need to establish your first apartment?_____ Is this a reasonable amount to expect to put out at the beginning of your marriage? Which items could you do without, and how much would you save?

Adults are responsible for many financial matters, and if they spend more money than they are capable of paying the results can be disastrous—even to the point of bankruptcy. Here are several items which you may wish to research on your own if you do not know how they are handled. The newly married couple, because their marriage is a matter of public record, will receive many attractive offers from high-pressure salesmen encouraging them to make purchases beyond which the couple is capable of repaying. What do you know about:

Life insurance
Different kinds of
  savings accounts
Bank services
Purchasing an automobile

Entering into a contract
Investing
Buying insurance
Purchasing a home
Paying taxes

An excellent resource which may help you in many areas, including budgeting is Jerome B. Cohen, *Personal Finance: Principles and Case Problems* (Homewood, Illinois: Richard D. Irwin, 1975).

"Everything in Its Place"

Using the furniture from the first exercise you are going to furnish your first apartment. Below you will find a diagram of a two-bedroom apartment. How would you arrange the furniture? If you are engaged, after you have completed your diagram compare your interior decorating ability with that of your fiancé.

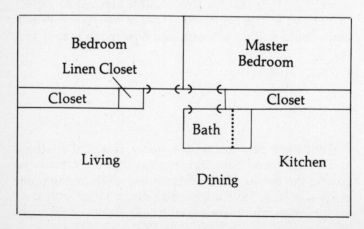

Whose decisions won out? How were the decisions made? Were you and your partner close or miles apart in your estimated cost of furnishing your first apartment?

NOTES

Chapter 9

Enriching Your Dating Life

DATING ATTITUDES SURVEY

To help you determine your present position in dating behavior and thinking about marriage, rate your attitudes and behaviors on the basis of the following scale:

DN   Definitely Not
PN   Probably Not
U   Unsure
PY   Probably Yes
DY   Definitely Yes

_____ 1. I would date a non-Christian if I had the opportunity.

_____ 2. I would go steady with a non-Christian if I had the opportunity.

_____ 3. I would marry a non-Christian if I had the opportunity.

_____ 4. I have dated a non-Christian.

_____ 5. I have dated more than one non-Christian.

_____ 6. I have often dated non-Christians.

_____ 7. I have gone steady with a non-Christian.

_____ 8. I have gone steady with more than one non-Christian.

_____ 9. I prefer dating non-Christians.

_____ 10. My parents don't care if I date non-Christians.

_____ 11. My parents don't care if I go steady with non-Christians.

_____ 12. My parents wouldn't care if I married a non-Christian.

_____ 13. My parents like me to date non-Christians.

—————14. My parents like me to go steady with non-Christians.

—————15. My parents would like it if I married a non-Christian.

Think about the following questions and write your answers on page 102.

1. What potential problems can you identify for a Christian dating a non-Christian?

2. What positive experiences might a person have by dating a non-Christian?

3. How do you feel about dating a non-Christian at this point in your life?

4. How do your parents feel about your dating a non-Christian?

Ideas for Enriching Your Dating Life

It is important that every couple learn to develop a number of interests and activities to enrich their marriage. Couples who have few or no mutual interests have little or no basis for enjoying their leisure time. To repeat the same dating activities week after week tends to limit the amount of interaction between the partners. Even though the activities are interesting and enjoyable, it may be hard to discover whether or not the partner is actually interesting or enjoyable. Couples who have a good marriage are couples who enjoy their leisure time together and who cooperate in their recreational adventures.

Below are listed numerous dating activites which can be engaged in by couples in most locales. You are encouraged to add to the list and also to add specific names of locations and places in your geographical area. Read through the entire list, then go through and check off the activities you have already engaged in. Then check off the activities you enjoy. Finally, check off the activities you would like to learn. If you are dating, which activities would you feel are appropriate for a date? What could you learn about your dating partner through that activity?

	Have Engaged In	Enjoy	Want to Try	Date	Could Learn
RECREATION					
Amusement parks	_____	____	____	____	____
Parks in general	_____	____	____	____	____
Movies	_____	____	____	____	____
Television	_____	____	____	____	____
Dancing	_____	____	____	____	____
Parties	_____	____	____	____	____
Visiting friends	_____	____	____	____	____
Visiting families	_____	____	____	____	____
Picnics	_____	____	____	____	____
Attending sports events					
Football	_____	____	____	____	____
Soccer	_____	____	____	____	____
Baseball	_____	____	____	____	____
Hockey	_____	____	____	____	____
Basketball	_____	____	____	____	____
Tennis matches	_____	____	____	____	____
COMMUNITY ACTIVITIES					
Visit a courtroom	_____	____	____	____	____
Work on an election campaign	_____	____	____	____	____
Join a civic club	_____	____	____	____	____
Volunteer work in a local agency					
Hospital	_____	____	____	____	____
Juvenile home	_____	____	____	____	____
Retirement home	_____	____	____	____	____
Convalescent hospital	_____	____	____	____	____
Halfway house	_____	____	____	____	____

	Have Engaged In	Enjoy	Want to Try	Date	Could Learn
City council meeting	___	___	___	___	___
Scouting	___	___	___	___	___

HOBBIES

Almost anything listed can serve as a hobby activity.

	Have Engaged In	Enjoy	Want to Try	Date	Could Learn
Collecting	___	___	___	___	___
Photography	___	___	___	___	___
Painting	___	___	___	___	___
Crafts	___	___	___	___	___

DINING

Try some new dining cuisines. Try to eat in at least one restaurant that offers each of the following styles of food:

	Have Engaged In	Enjoy	Want to Try	Date	Could Learn
American	___	___	___	___	___
Armenian	___	___	___	___	___
Basque	___	___	___	___	___
Brazilian	___	___	___	___	___
Chinese	___	___	___	___	___
Continental	___	___	___	___	___
English	___	___	___	___	___
European	___	___	___	___	___
French	___	___	___	___	___
German	___	___	___	___	___
Greek	___	___	___	___	___
Indian	___	___	___	___	___
Japanese	___	___	___	___	___
Italian	___	___	___	___	___

	Have Engaged In	Enjoy	Want to Try	Date	Could Learn
Jewish	___	___	___	___	___
Mexican	___	___	___	___	___
Middle Eastern	___	___	___	___	___
Oriental	___	___	___	___	___
Polynesian	___	___	___	___	___
Russian	___	___	___	___	___
Scandinavian	___	___	___	___	___
Soul food	___	___	___	___	___
Spanish	___	___	___	___	___
Swiss	___	___	___	___	___

SPORTS EVENTS

	Have Engaged In	Enjoy	Want to Try	Date	Could Learn
Tennis	___	___	___	___	___
Skiing					
Alpine	___	___	___	___	___
Cross-country	___	___	___	___	___
Backpacking	___	___	___	___	___
Bicycling	___	___	___	___	___
Hiking	___	___	___	___	___
Fishing	___	___	___	___	___
Horseback riding	___	___	___	___	___
Rock climbing	___	___	___	___	___
Boating					
Kayaking	___	___	___	___	___
Canoeing	___	___	___	___	___
Sailing	___	___	___	___	___
Motorboating	___	___	___	___	___
Skin diving	___	___	___	___	___
Scuba diving	___	___	___	___	___
Golf	___	___	___	___	___
Swimming	___	___	___	___	___
Jogging	___	___	___	___	___
Hunting	___	___	___	___	___
Skydiving	___	___	___	___	___
Motorcycling	___	___	___	___	___

	Have Engaged In	Enjoy	Want to Try	Date	Could Learn
Camping	____	____	____	____	____
Bowling	____	____	____	____	____
Roller skating	____	____	____	____	____
Ice skating	____	____	____	____	____
Waterskiing	____	____	____	____	____
Handball	____	____	____	____	____
Racquetball	____	____	____	____	____
Volleyball	____	____	____	____	____

CULTURAL EVENTS

	Have Engaged In	Enjoy	Want to Try	Date	Could Learn
Theater	____	____	____	____	____
Musicals	____	____	____	____	____
Ballet	____	____	____	____	____
Horse shows	____	____	____	____	____
Dog shows	____	____	____	____	____
Museums					
Natural history	____	____	____	____	____
Science	____	____	____	____	____
Art	____	____	____	____	____
Historical	____	____	____	____	____
Planetarium	____	____	____	____	____
Observatory	____	____	____	____	____
Opera	____	____	____	____	____
Photo exhibits	____	____	____	____	____
Religious pageants	____	____	____	____	____
Concerts					
Jazz	____	____	____	____	____
Rock	____	____	____	____	____
Folk	____	____	____	____	____
Country	____	____	____	____	____
Symphony	____	____	____	____	____
Classical	____	____	____	____	____
Chamber	____	____	____	____	____
Garden show	____	____	____	____	____

	Have Engaged In	Enjoy	Want to Try	Date	Could Learn
County fair	___	___	___	___	___
Zoos	___	___	___	___	___
Animal parks	___	___	___	___	___
Botanical gardens	___	___	___	___	___

EDUCATIONAL ACTIVITIES

	Have Engaged In	Enjoy	Want to Try	Date	Could Learn
Lectures					
Travel	___	___	___	___	___
Art	___	___	___	___	___
Gardening	___	___	___	___	___
Political	___	___	___	___	___
Health	___	___	___	___	___
Food	___	___	___	___	___
Formal classes	___	___	___	___	___
Lessons in almost anything	___	___	___	___	___
Music lessons	___	___	___	___	___
Singing	___	___	___	___	___
Attending an auction	___	___	___	___	___
Collecting					
Stamps	___	___	___	___	___
Coins	___	___	___	___	___
Antiques	___	___	___	___	___
Bottles	___	___	___	___	___
Nostalgia in general	___	___	___	___	___

CHURCH ACTIVITIES

	Have Engaged In	Enjoy	Want to Try	Date	Could Learn
Worship	___	___	___	___	___
Sunday school	___	___	___	___	___
Choir	___	___	___	___	___
Conferences	___	___	___	___	___

	Have Engaged In	Enjoy	Want to Try	Date	Could Learn
Camps	___	___	___	___	___
Retreats	___	___	___	___	___
Growth groups	___	___	___	___	___
Prayer meetings	___	___	___	___	___
Teaching a class together	___	___	___	___	___
Fellowship activities	___	___	___	___	___
Evangelism	___	___	___	___	___
Visitation	___	___	___	___	___
Volunteer work	___	___	___	___	___

List the top ten activities you would like to participate in on a date:

1. _____   6. _____

2. _____   7. _____

3. _____   8. _____

4. _____   9. _____

5. _____   10. _____

Besides being fun, what other benefits could you derive in terms of getting to know another person more deeply through engaging in the activities listed on the previous pages?

What other kinds of dates have not been mentioned? These may be peculiar to your local area or climate. List them below:

1. _____ 4. _____

2. _____ 5. _____

3. _____ 6. _____

Describe the most interesting date you ever had.

One idea for enriching your dating life would be to combine two or more activities into a "super date"— that is, visiting a museum and then having dinner at a special restaurant. Below describe your idea of the ideal date.

NOTES

Chapter 10
How to Say No
or How to Resist Saying Yes

As much as we would like to be able to say yes to most everything, we have neither the time nor the resources to do all the things that are demanded of us. It is necessary for us to refuse to do some things that we would like to do and it is often necessary to refuse to do things that we would not like to do.

If you are a female, there may be a mother in your neighborhood who expects you to babysit on 5 minutes notice for half the price you normally get. You do this out of fear of offending your mother or her friends or out of concern that you may not be hired by other parents in the neighborhood. You may have a part-time job, and the boss requests that you stay a few minutes past your scheduled quitting time. This goes on over a period of time until you may be spending several extra hours a month at work for which you are not receiving pay and you are afraid to speak up for fear of losing your job.

How then do you say no? Whether it is to a parent, an employer, a friend, a date, your fiancé, or your husband or wife. Below are several rules which should be observed when you find it necessary to make a polite or firm refusal:

1. It is important to practice your refusal if you have the opportunity beforehand. If not, you can anticipate situations that might necessitate a refusal by discussing them with others. Most things that we do well we accomplish through practice.
2. Be careful where you express your refusal. Don't tell someone you won't go steady with him in front

of a crowd of his best friends. Choose a time and place that will not embarrass either you or the other person.

3. You may want to answer the following questions before verbalizing your refusal.
    a. What feelings am I experiencing?
    b. What do I want to accomplish with my refusal?
    c. What are some possible negative responses from the other person, and how could I answer them?

4. If you are experiencing depression, guilt, or insecurity, it may be good for you to postpone saying yes or no until you find yourself in a better frame of mind.

5. Don't be afraid to say no. Both you and the other person will be able to survive.

Planning Worksheet Information

Once a decision has been made, whether to say no, or to buy a car, or whatever, there are four steps which you must take in order to see the completion of that decision.

The first thing that must be established is to identify the area or objective you are concerned with. It may be:

1. Developing a dating standard
2. Planning for college
3. Planning the wedding
4. Having a child
5. Etc.

Step number one is "Forecasting" and includes evaluating where you are currently and then determining where you will be if the present course continues without any changes. It also includes knowing why you are involved in that situation. An example of an area of consideration might be your physical relationship with your dating partner. "Where I am" might be to define the extent to which you are currently involved physically with your dating partner. "The reason I may be expressing myself to this extent" could be due to the pressure which has been placed on you by your family and friends. The *second step* that needs to be taken is that of setting objectives. Questions that should be asked could include: What is to be accomplished? Where will it take place? When should it occur? Using the above example a person may decide that, "He has become too involved physically with another individual and his objective is to decrease his involvement with . . ." "Where it will take place" might be that he will no longer park with the other person on lovers' lane. The "when" might be "beginning today." The *third step* is that of programming or deciding the specific number and nature of steps that are necessary to meet your objective. Then it is necessary to arrange each step in order of priority and ask the following questions:

1. Will this step help me to meet my objective? Is it the best step possible?
2. Are there any prerequisites that must be met to accomplish each step?

The next part of programming is that of assessing your strengths which will aid you in completing your objectives, and identifying the obstacles that must be overcome.

The *final step* is to establish a timetable for completing each step in your objective and setting a date for the completion of the objective.

At this time use the Planning Worksheet below and evaluate your current dating standards and develop the standard you would like to follow in the future.

Worksheet

Area of consideration _____

I. Forecasting:
   A. "Where am I?" _____
   B. "Why am I here?" _____

II. Setting objectives: "What will I do?" _____
   A. "What is to be accomplished?" _____
   B. "Where will it take place?" _____
   C. "When should it occur?" _____

III. Programming: "How will I do it?" _____
   A. "Is the relation of the steps to the objective close?" _____

B. "What are the prerequisites?"_____

C. "What strengths do I possess to accomplish this?" _____

D. "What obstacles need to be overcome?"_____ _____

IV. Establishing a timetable for completion of each step.

Step No.	Description of the Steps in the Process of the Project	Schedule	
		Start	End
1			
2			
3			
4			
5			
6			

After finishing the worksheet go back and reread the five rules for making a refusal.

Play Solomon

Use the note page to write down your response to each of the case studies.

Phil and Cathy have been going together since junior high school. They have gotten along well together and have only had a few disagreements. They are now seniors in high school and are thinking very seriously about getting married right after graduation. Phil has the opportunity to get into the Teamsters Union and drive a truck. They tell him though that the work is seasonal but after a few years he will be able to work all year long. He also has the opportunity to go to college, but that will mean Cathy will have to work. Cathy's parents aren't too excited about the marriage plans but indicated that they would be willing to pay for Phil's schooling as long as he got good grades. What possible problems do you see for Phil and Cathy? What would you say to them?

Steve and Jerri met at summer camp where they both worked. They have dated casually for the two summers that they have worked on the summer staff and have seen each other at Christmas and Easter vacations in between. Jerri lives in Seattle, while Steve lives in San Diego. Both are juniors in college and are planning to be teachers. At this time they are considering marriage but aren't quite sure. They still have some doubts. They have heard of you and have come for some advice. What will you tell them?

Tom and Pat went to high school together. They dated seriously during their senior year, and when Tom received a scholarship to study in England, he presented Pat with an engagement ring the night they graduated from high school. Pat's parents are really in favor of the marriage and expect them to marry as soon as Tom graduates from college. Tom and Pat have not seen each other during the last three years except for one week last summer. Pat's parents have already made the wedding plans for this summer, as Tom will graduate and be returning to the states. Pat appears to be excited and has helped her mother with the wedding plans. Tom has not really said much of anything, even in his letters, except that he is planning to go through with the wedding. Tom and Pat are your best friends. What advice would you like to share with them?

NOTES

Chapter 11

How We Communicate (Part I)

Communication—it's a big word and an important word. Consider this fact: If there is no communication there is no relationship—with your parents, your fiancé or dating partner, with God. Communication is a must! Someone said, "Communication is to love what blood is to the body."

You are a communicator. But what do you communicate, and how do you do it? What messages are you sending to others? Do your messages get through? Let's rate your communication and discover what you believe. Rate the communication between you and your parents on this scale of 0 to 10 (0 being the worst and 10 the best):

| 0 | 1 | 2 | 3 | 4 | 5 | 6 | 7 | 8 | 9 | 10 |

Now indicate how you think your parents would rate the communication between them and you.

| 0 | 1 | 2 | 3 | 4 | 5 | 6 | 7 | 8 | | 10 |

Now rate the communication between you and your fiancé or dating partner.

| 0 | 1 | 2 | 3 | 4 | 5 | 6 | 7 | 8 | 9 | 10 |

Where does our communication come from? If we have communication problems do they stem from the words or from what is behind them? Actually, what we say or share is simply a reflection of what we have been thinking and feeling.

If our words are creating problems in our communication, let's go back to our thought life and evaluate the contents. Jesus said, "Listen, and understand this thoroughly! It is not what goes into a man's mouth that makes him common or unclean. It is what comes out of a man's mouth that makes him unclean . . . Don't you see that whatever goes into the mouth passes into the stomach and then out of the body altogether? But the things that come out of a man's mouth come from his heart and mind, and it is they that really make a man unclean. For it is from a man's mind that evil thoughts arise—murder, adultery, lust, theft, perjury and blasphemy" (Matt. 15: 10-20, Phillips).

The transition from mind to mouth sometimes breaks down because the words we use do not correctly convey our message. Do you always mean what you say or say what you mean?

Try this experiment. Write down ten to fifteen of the most frequent phrases you use with your family and your partner, and do the same with the phrases that your partner uses. Give your fiancé or dating partner the list of phrases or words that you use and ask him to write down what he thinks they mean. Write down what you think his phrases or words mean. Then compare!

1._____

2._____

3._____

4._____

5._____

6._____

7._____

8. _____

9. _____

10. _____

11. _____

12. _____

13. _____

14. _____

15. _____

Before we proceed, define the word *communication*.

When you have written your definition, ask your mom, dad or a friend how he would define the word, and then compare.

Now let's define the word *listening*.

What do the following passages say about listening?
Matthew 11:15; 13:9, 43

Proverbs 18:13

James 1:23

Listening Evaluation

Describe a time that you were really listened to. How did you feel?

Describe a time when someone didn't listen to you. How did you feel?

How can others tell that you are really listening to them? (To verify your answer, ask another person how he can tell.)

"How I Listen"

1. What do I think my fiancé or dating partner is thinking about when I talk to him?

2. How can you tell nonverbally that your fiancé or dating partner listens to you? How can he tell if you are listening to him?

3. What words or verbal response do you use to let your fiancé or dating partner know that you are listening?

4. When I really want to listen to my fiancé or dating partner I :

5. When I don't want to listen to my fiancé or dating partner I usually :

6. When my fiancé or dating partner really listens to me I feel :

7. The time that I have felt that God really listened :

8. The time that I have felt that I really listened to God was :

NOTES

Chapter 12

How We Communicate (Part II)

What does the Word of God have to say about communication? Have you ever considered what the book of Proverbs says about communication? Let's take some time to search through these passages. As you read each one, write down the result of this type of speech or communication. The passage and main theme of the verse has been given to you. After you have completed this study, try to categorize the verses. You might use headings such as "think before you speak," "talking too much," "timing," "speak the truth," "the power of our words," "nagging," etc.

Proverbs	Theme	Result
4:24	False, willful, and contrary talk	_____
6:12	Perverse mouth	_____
10:18	Hatred, slander	_____
10:19	Too many words	_____
10:19	Restrains lips	_____
11:9a	Destruction of neighbor	_____
11:12a	Belittles	_____
11:12	Silence	_____
12:16	Ignore insult	_____
12:18a	Rash speech	_____
12:18	Wise tongue	_____
12:22	Truth	_____
12:22	Lies	_____
12:25	Encouraging word	_____

Proverbs	Theme	Result
13:3	Guards mouth	_____
14:23	Idle talk	_____
15:1	Soft answer	_____
15:4	Gentle tongue	_____
15:23	Apt answer—timing	_____
16:24	Pleasant words	_____
16:27-28	Strife, whisperer	_____
17:9	Nagging	_____
17:27-28	Spare words	_____
18:4	Wise—deep	_____
18:6-7	Fool's lips	_____
18:8	Talebearer	_____
18:13	Listens first	_____
19:11	Restrains anger	_____
19:11	Overlook offense	_____
20:3	Cease from strife	_____
20:25	Vow	_____
21:9	Listen first	_____
21:23	Guards mouth	_____
24:26	Straight answer	_____
24:28	Deception and lies	_____
25:15	Soft speech	_____
25:24	Nagging	_____
26:22-23	Lies, gossip	_____
26:28	Lying, flatter	_____
28:23	Rebuke	_____
29:5	Flatters	_____
29:11	Holds back anger	_____
29:11	Lets out all anger	_____
29:20	Hasty	_____
29:22	Wrath and anger	_____

1. Which of these passages should be employed in our communication?

2. Select the characteristics that you need to exhibit more in the way you communicate with your parents, then with your fiancé or dating partner.

3. Select the characteristics that you feel your parents and/or fiancé or dating partner needs to exhibit more in the way he communicates.

Earlier we talked about the meaning behind words. Your words (as you have probably seen by now in Proverbs) have tremendous power. List three things you can do to improve communication between yourself and your parents, fiancé or dating partner. "I plan to improve our communication by:"

1. _____

2. _____

3. _____

I will start doing these three things (date)_____ at (time)_____."

If you had to teach someone what styles of communication to avoid, what characteristics would you mention? Let's think of these as blocks to good communication. Listed on the following page are a number of communication blocks. Select what you think are the ten main problems and list them in order of importance.

Communication Blockers

1._____   6._____

2._____   7._____

3._____   8._____

4._____   9._____

5._____   10._____

Not listening

Not saying what you
  really mean

Defensiveness

Arguments

Surface talk

Emotional talk

No eye contact

Shifting the topic

Nagging

Silence

Monotone

Big or abstract words

Speaking for the other
  person

Yelling

Put downs

Faces the other direction
  when talking

Refuses to talk

Quarrels

Uses inflamatory words

Complaining

Levels of Communication

Let's say that you do talk. You do communicate. But what do you communicate? What is it like? Is it simple or profound, factual or emotional? Consider this classification of communication styles from John Powell's book, *Why Am I Afraid to Tell You Who I Am?* We communicate on five different levels, from shallow cliches to deep personal comments. Hang-ups, such as fear, apathy, or a poor self-image keep us at the shallow level. If we can be freed from our restrictions, we can move to the deeper, more meaningful level. The five levels of communication are:

Level Five: Cliche Conversation. This type of talk is

very safe. We use words such as "How are you?" "How's the dog?" "Where have you been?" "I like your dress." In this type of conversation there is no personal sharing. Each person remains safely behind his defenses.

Level Four: Reporting the Facts about Others. In this kind of conversation we are content to tell others what someone else has said, but we offer no personal information on these facts. We report the facts like the six o'clock news. We share gossip and little narrations but we do not commit ourselves as to how we feel about it.

Level Three: My Ideas and Judgments. Real communication begins to unfold here. The person is willing to step out of his solitary confinement and risk telling some of his ideas and decisions. He is still cautious. If he senses what he is saying is not being accepted, he will retreat.

Level Two: My Feelings (Emotions). At this level the person shares how he feels about facts, ideas, and judgments. His feelings underneath these areas are revealed. For a person to really share himself with another individual he must move to the level of sharing his feelings.

Level One: Complete Emotional and Personal Communication. All deep relationships must be based on absolute openness and honesty. This may be difficult to achieve because it involves risk—the risk of being rejected. But it is vital if relationships are to grow. There will be times when this type of communication is not as complete as it could be. [1]

Take the time right now and write down your answer to these questions:

1. What are some of the reasons why a person might respond only at level five or level four?

2. When do you feel most like responding at levels two and one?

3. At which level do you usually respond?

4. At which level do your family members usually respond?

5. At which level would you like your dates to respond?

6. At which level do you usually communicate with God?

7. At what level should a couple be when they
   a. start to date?

   b. date regularly?

   c. go steady?

   d. promise to marry? (engaged to be engaged)

   e. become engaged?

   f. marry?

It is important that our messages be true to our meaning in order for us to be understood and to understand others. Too many people give bent messages or stero messages—speaking out of both sides of their mouth at the same time. The Word of God says that we are to "speak the truth in love" (Ephesians 4:26).

To make sure that your message means what you want it to mean, check your tone of voice and your nonverbal behavior. These two factors are truer indicators of what you mean and feel than the actual words you use. If you say to your partner that you're really interested in what he did on a certain day, and you say it in a flat tone of voice with your head buried behind a magazine, will he really believe you? Would you believe it? One researcher stated that the actual words we use in our face-to-face conversation makes up only 7 percent of our message while the tone of voice accounts for 38 percent and the nonverbal aspect 55 percent.[2]

If this is true, what is our tone of voice saying to the other person? If we claim that we are in control and are not angry, is our tone a giveaway? What does our body posture say to our fiancé or dating partner as we talk? Do we slouch, stand with hands on hips, slam the cupboards as we talk to him, cross our arms, turn our back on him, or raise our eyebrows when we ask a question? All of these behaviors and actions send a message.

How would you handle the following communication problems? Read each case and then write (1) how you would feel and (2) what you would do to resolve the problem.

1. Your fiancé, dating partner or a family member uses a word or phrase that irritates you. Whenever you hear this word or phrase you get upset and react angrily. It is almost as though the other person wants you to get into a quarrel. What could you do so that you don't react in this manner? How could you avoid getting upset and drawn into a quarrel? What could you do to help yourself if this is your pattern?

2. Your fiancé, dating partner or a family member uses silence when he is upset. He refuses to talk with you and at times it seems to you that he is punishing you with his silence. What can you do to help him to talk with you?

What could you do to help yourself if this is your pattern?

3. Your fiancé, dating partner or a family member seems to talk on a superficial level only. He doesn't really share deep thoughts with you. He doesn't talk about what he really believes or feels. What could you do to help him?

What could you do to help yourself if this is your pattern?

4. Your fiancé, dating partner or a family member uses sarcasm and criticism. You feel like your character is being assassinated. What could you do to help change

this? What could you say to him so he would really understand how you feel about it?

What could you do to help yourself if this is your pattern?

5. Your fiancé, dating partner or a family member has a strong tendency to become defensive when you talk to him about a problem or even make a neutral statement. What could you suggest here?

What could you do to help yourself if this is your pattern?

6. Your fiancé, dating partner or a family member makes nice or kind statements, but his facial expression doesn't convey the same thought or feeling. Some of his behaviors also do not correspond with what he has said to you. He tells you he loves you, but you don't see any

follow-through. What could you do to help bring about a change?

What could you do to help yourself if this is your pattern?

7. Your fiancé, dating partner or a family member has a tendency to lie. Not just straight-out lies but devious untruths. You are having a hard time trying to figure out what he is really asking when he asks you questions. It seems that his questions are untruthful as well. You feel hesitant to answer his questions because if you are truthful he seems to get really upset. What could you do about this problem?

What could you do to help yourself if this is your pattern?

8. Your fiancé, dating partner or a family member is nicknamed "Chief Running Mouth." He never seems to stop talking. On and on he goes about anything. And if

there has been a problem, he really gets on your case. What could you do?

What could you do to help yourself if this is your pattern?

9. Your fiancé, dating partner or a family member doesn't think before he speaks. He just blurts it out. But later, he says he is sorry and claims that's just the way he is. He just doesn't think until after he's said it and you'll just have to accept him the way he is. What could you do to help him?

What could you do to help yourself if this is your pattern?

References

1. John Powell, *Why Am I Afraid to Tell You Who I Am?* (Chicago: Argus Communications, 1969), pp. 54-62.

2. Albert Metowbian, *Silent Messages* (Belmont, Calif.: Wadsworth Publishing Co., 1971), pp. 42-44.

NOTES

Chapter 13

Conflict (or "The Fight Is On!")

Have you ever experienced conflict? Of course you have. Everyone has at one time or another. How you respond to conflict and what you let it do to you is very important.

1. What are the typical conflicts that couples experience when they are:

   a. starting to date?

   b. going steady?

   c. engaged?

   d. married?

2. Describe the conflicts that you have experienced, if you have been at any of these stages, and describe how you have handled them.

3. Describe how your parents have handled conflict. What have you learned from them that you would like to bring into your own marriage?

4. What effect do you think the emotion anger has upon conflict?

How do you handle anger?

What angers you the most?

Anger is a strong, usually temporary displeasure. You can be just as angry while keeping silent as you can while yelling at someone.

The words *rage* and *fury* are used to describe intense, uncontained, explosive emotion. Fury is thought of as being destructive, but rage can be considered justified by certain circumstances. Have you seen either of these emotions in yourself?

Another word for anger is *wrath*—fervid anger that seeks vengeance or punishment. *Resentment* is usually used to signify suppressed anger brought about by a sense of grievance. *Indignation* is a feeling which results when you see the mistreatment of someone or something that is very important to you.

A simple definition of anger is a strong feeling of irritation or displeasure.

The Word of God has much to say about anger and uses a number of words to describe the various types of anger. In the Old Testament the word for anger actually meant "nostril" or "nose." In ancient Hebrew psychology the nose was thought to be the seat of anger. The phrase "slow to anger" literally means "long of nose."

Synonyms used in the Old Testament for anger include ill-humor and rage (Esther 1:12), overflowing rage and fury (Amos 1:11), and indignation (Jer. 15:17). The emotion of anger can be the subject of the scripture even though the exact word is not present. Anger can be implied through words such as revenge, cursing, jealousy, snorting, trembling, shouting, raving, and grinding the teeth.

What do the following verses have to say about the right way to handle anger?

1. Psalm 37:1-11

2. Proverbs 14:29

3. Proverbs 15:1

4. Proverbs 15:28

5. Proverbs 16:32

6. Proverbs 19:11

7. Proverbs 25:28

8. Proverbs 29:11

9. Matthew 5:43-44

10. Romans 8:28-29

11. Romans 12:19-21

12. Galatians 5:16-23

13. Ephesians 4:26

14. Ephesians 4:29

15. Ephesians 4:32

16. 1 Peter 3:9

What causes conflicts? See James 4:1-3

A Look at Your Relationships

1. Describe a recent or current conflict between you and your fiancé or dating partner.

2. What do you believe caused the conflict? What was the outcome? What did it accomplish?

3. How did you create or contribute to the conflict?

4. Imagine that you are seeing the conflict from the other person's perspective. How would your fiancé or dating partner describe the conflict?

5. What could you do to resolve the conflict?

6. List some of the issues you and your parents, fiancé or dating partner disagree on that do not need to be completely resolved.

7. What does "completely resolved" mean to you?

8. Make a list of some issues on which you disagree that do need a solution.

9. Select one of the issues on which more time needs to be spent. Write an explanation of the situation— as you see it.

10. What choices does a person have in resolving conflicts? Here are five suggested ways of resolving them.

CONFLICT RESOLUTION

Yield	Resolve
Compromise	
Withdraw	Win

1. Describe what you think withdraw means.

2. Describe what you think yield means.

3. Describe what you think compromise means.

4. Describe what you think win means.

5. Describe what you think resolve means.

   Now go back to each of these and rate them with the following rating:

   1. Which show a high concern for a person's relationship?

2. Which show a low concern for a person's relationship?

3. Which style might be low in helping you meet your needs?

4. Which style might be high in helping you meet your needs?

Now that you rated the above relationships, please do the following:

1. Select your usual style of dealing with conflicts.

2. Select your parents' style of dealing with conflicts.

3. Select your fiancé or dating partner's usual style of dealing with conflicts.

4. Describe a situation at home or on a date when you withdrew from a conflict. How did this affect you and the other person?

5. Describe a situation in which you won a conflict at home or with your fiancé or dating partner. How did this affect you and the other person?

6. Describe a situation in which you yielded in a conflict either at home or on a date. How did this affect you and the other person?

7. Describe a situation in which you compromised in a conflict either at home or on a date. How did this affect you and the other person?

8. Describe a situation in which you resolved a conflict at home or on a date. How did this affect you and the other person?

What do the following scriptures say about the various styles which you have just considered?
Genesis 4 (Cain and Abel)

1 Samuel 20:30-34

Matthew 15:10-20

Mark 11:11-19

Luke 23:18-25

John 8:1-11

John 11:11-19

What principles or plan could you develop and follow in order to resolve conflicts? Describe in detail in the space provided.

NOTES

NOTES

Chapter 14

What Is Sex?

What is Sex and What do I Believe About Sex?

Answer the following questions:

1. Sex is _____

_____

2. The word *sex* actually means _____

_____

3. Girls and women think sex is _____

_____

4. Boys and men think sex is _____

_____

5. The Bible teaches that sex is _____

_____

6. The Bible has more negative things to say about sex than positive. Agree or disagree?

7. Young men are normally girl watchers. Young women are not normally man watchers. Agree or disagree?

8. If I had the opportunity to ask any questions that I ever wanted to ask about sex, they would be _____

_____

_____

_____

_____

_____

_____

Where I Learned about Sex

1. From what source did you first learn the basic facts about sex and reproduction? Can you remember how you felt about what you heard?

2. What was the first negative statement you ever heard about sex and from whom?

3. What was the first positive statement you ever heard about sex and from whom?

4. During the past few years did you have anyone with whom you felt comfortable when talking about your questions concerning sex? If so, who was it?

5. Do you think there is too much emphasis upon sex today? Why or why not? What are the reasons for your answer?

6. Are there any questions or topics that you would hesitate in asking your parents concerning sex? If so, what questions and why?

7. Do you feel that you know enough about the meaning and purpose of sex for:
   a. dating?
   b. engagement?
   c. marriage?
   If not, what else do you need to know?

NOTES

NOTES

NOTES

Chapter 15
Sexual Behavior and the Word of God

Earlier in this workbook we talked about the idea of intimacy. Often people associate sex with being intimate. But there is a difference. There are different types of intimacy. There is also a difference between sex and love. Some people say that they have loved another person when they have had sex with him. But that isn't necessarily true. Many people have sexual intercourse, but love has nothing to do with what went on. Notice here the differences between love and sex.

DIFFERENCES BETWEEN LOVE AND SEX	
LOVE . . .	*SEX . . .*
. . . is a process; you must go through it to understand what it is.	. . . is static; you have some idea of what it is like prior to going through it.
. . . is a learned operation; you must learn what to do through first having been loved and cared for by someone.	. . . is known naturally; you know instinctively what to do.
. . . requires constant attention.	. . . takes no effort.
. . . experiences slow growth—takes time to develop and evolve.	. . . is very fast—needs no time to develop.
. . . is deepened by creative thinking.	. . . is controlled mostly by feel—that is, responding to stimuli.
. . . is many small behavior changes that bring about good feelings.	. . . is one big feeling brought about by one big behavior.

LOVE . . .	SEX . . .
. . . is an act of will with or without good feelings—sometimes "Don't feel like it."	. . . is an act of will—you feel like it.
. . . involves the respect of the person to develop.	. . . does not require the respect of the person.
. . . is lots of warm laughter.	. . . is little or no laughter.
. . . requires knowing how to thoughtfully interact, to talk, to develop interesting conversations.	. . . requires little or no talking.
. . . develops in depth to sustain the relationship, involves much effort, where eventually real happiness is to be found.	. . . promises permanent relationship but never happens, can't sustain relationship, forever feature is an illusion.

What do you believe about expressing your affection for another person in a physical manner? There are many standards today (and lack of standards). First, think about this question and then write your answer:

What is the purpose of expressing your affection toward another person in a physical way?

My Standard of Sexual Expression

In the space provided, describe or depict your standard that you have established for expressing your affection toward your fiancé or dating partner. In each state indicate the types of physical expression that you would like to feel is okay to express.

Friendship	Dating	Going Steady	Engagement	Marriage

Purpose of Sexual Activity

What is the purpose of sexual activity? Write out your response.

Letha Scanzoni suggested that the purpose of sexual activity is fourfold—procreation, recreation, communication, and release. She described these aspects as follows:

"Procreation

"Sex is the vehicle God designed for babies to come into the world. It was the way He planned the human race to reproduce itself. This is the most obvious function of sex, but it is not the *only* function . . .

"The reproductive aspect of sex is mentioned at the very outset of creation. Just as God had commanded the fish and birds to be fruitful and multiply (Genesis 1:22), so He commanded man and woman (Genesis 1:28) to the end that the earth should be filled. Sex for procreation is also seen in Deuteronomy 7:13, 14, where God's people were told that faithfulness to His covenant and obedience to His commandment would result in human, animal, and plant fertility.

"Likewise the Psalms are full of references to the procreational side of sex. Psalm 127:3 calls children a heritage of the Lord and 'the fruit of the womb a reward.' . . .

"And so it is throughout the Scriptures and throughout human history. Procreation is a very important purpose of sex. But it is by no means the only purpose . . .

"Recreation

"At first many Christians may be shocked to learn that sex is for fun and recreation and that the Scriptures actually encourage the enjoyment and sensual delights of sex.

". . . for the Christian couple, sex can be regarded as sacred—if by this we mean set apart for God—desirous of pleasing and experiencing God's blessing in our sex life as well as in every area of life . . .

"It will be helpful to note that the Bible writers often used poetic language to describe sexual organs, drives, energies, desires, and outlets. A favorite symbol for sex in Scripture is water—fountains, streams, cisterns, springs, and wells. In Proverbs 5 the human desire for sexual pleasure is clearly recognized. But the young man who is being addressed is told that he must find this pleasure only in marriage, only with his wife . . .

"Communication

"In the marriage relationship, sexual intercourse was also designed by God to provide a means of expressing the deep unity a husband and wife feel toward one another. There can also be a communion of spirits when there is a union of bodies. This may very well be why the Bible writers frequently used the word 'know' when referring to sexual intercourse. See, for example, Genesis 4:1, where we're told that 'Adam knew Eve his wife, and she conceived.'

"Release

"The fourth aspect of sex mentioned in the Bible has to do with sheer bodily release. The physical nature of sexual drives, tensions, and energies is very real, and the Scriptures recognize this. This is not to suggest that a life of celibacy is impossible, nor that sex must be seen as *the* all powerful force which drives our lives so that we're overwhelmed with passion and are helpless in resisting desire. The Bible has a great deal to say about self-control and God's enablement and strengthening in times of temptation."[1]

My Attitude Toward Sex

This is what John White has suggested:

"A Christian must bear three things in mind . . . First,

he must realize that God made his body (including the 'sexual' parts of it) and that he equipped it with a nervous system designed to enable each of us to experience exquisite pleasures, pleasures that anticipate the rapture our spirits will one day enjoy in a love-relationship with Christ.

"Second, pleasure is a by-product in life, not a goal. A hedonist is someone for whom pleasure is a guiding principle.

"Sigmund Freud saw man as a creature whose every action was controlled by the pursuit of pleasure and the avoidance of pain. Most of us have already discovered, however, that when we devote ourselves to pursuing pleasure, pleasure ceases to be a delight. Our appetites grow jaded and require ever more stimulation. On the other hand when we devote our lives to loving obedience to God and to serve one another, we find that the pleasure that eluded us when we made them our goal spring unbidden to surprise us. To seek pleasure is to find disenchantment. To seek God is to find (among other things) piercing pleasures.

"Third, sexual pleasure was designed to be enjoyed within marrige. The physical side of sex is only part of a larger whole. ". . . the first purpose of sex is the ending of isolation and loneliness. And loneliness can only end where trust exists—trust that someone has made a commitment to me and to that person in a sworn convenant until death parts us. Within such a relationship the physical pleasures of sex may blossom and mysteriously deepen to solidify the relationship."[2]

God's Attitude Toward Sexual Expression

Look up the following verses and summarize what you think the passages are saying.

Genesis 1:26-28

1 Timothy 4:4-5

Genesis 38:9

Deuteronomy 24:5

Proverbs 5:18-20

1 Corinthians 7:3, 4

Song of Solomon

What About My Body?
What does the Word of God have to say? Look up the following passages:
Psalm 139:13-17

Romans 12:1, 6:13

1 Corinthians 6:13, 14, 19, 20

What guidelines would you suggest for a person to follow in maintaining his standard of sexual expression? Suggest as many as you can.

References

1. Letha Scanzoni, *Sex Is a Parent Affair* (Glendale, Calif.: G/L Publications, 1973), pp. 16-21.

2. John White, *Eros Defiled* (Downers Grove, Ill.: InterVarsity Press, 1977), p. 11

NOTES

Chapter 16

You Are the One

After spending, in most cases, several years dating numerous people, for some usually unidentified reasons, we become attracted to one person with whom we spend the remainder of our lives. On the basis of the material presented in the sessions, the work that you have done on your own in this workbook, and discussions with your family, what are you looking for in a life partner?

Below are listed several exercises which you can use in helping to determine God's will for the choice of a life partner.

1. Describe the life partner that you are looking for (physical characteristics, intellectual capabilities, personality, and spiritual characteristics).

2. Is the person you described likely to be discovered by you in your circle of friends? What if this kind of individual is not likely to be among your acquaintances either present or future? What will you do to find him or her?

3. Would your parents be in agreement with you marrying the individual that you described in question number one? If not, why not?

4. How would you feel if God presented to you an individual with none of your ideals?

Checklist for Livable Family relationships

The ten statements printed below provide some practical guidelines for evaluating a relationship and for assisting you in deciding whether a person may be a suitable life partner. Each statement is followed by a rating scale from 1 (strongly disagree) to 10 (strongly agree). Place your initials on the scale where you see yourself responding to the statement.

1. We have the same general economic and social outlook on life.

Strongly Disagree				Don't Know				Strongly Agree	
1	2	3	4	5	6	7	8	9	10

2. He or she has the qualities I want to see in my children.

Strongly Disagree				Don't Know				Strongly Agree	
1	2	3	4	5	6	7	8	9	10

3. I have real respect for him or her.

Strongly Disagree				Don't Know				Strongly Agree	
1	2	3	4	5	6	7	8	9	10

4. This is the kind of person I want to look at across the breakfast table for the next forty years.

Strongly Disagree				Don't Know				Strongly Agree	
1	2	3	4	5	6	7	8	9	10

5. We get along well under pressure.

Strongly Disagree				Don't Know				Strongly Agree	
1	2	3	4	5	6	7	8	9	10

6. We communicate well.

Strongly Disagree				Don't Know				Strongly Agree	
1	2	3	4	5	6	7	8	9	10

7. I can really share myself with him or her.

Strongly Disagree				Don't Know				Strongly Agree	
1	2	3	4	5	6	7	8	9	10

8. I accept him or her as he or she is.

Strongly Disagree				Don't Know				Strongly Agree	
1	2	3	4	5	6	7	8	9	10

9. He or she accepts me as I am.

Strongly Disagree				Don't Know				Strongly Agree	
1	2	3	4	5	6	7	8	9	10

10. Neither of us has a desire to change the other to make him or her easier to love.

Strongly Disagree				Don't Know				Strongly Agree	
1	2	3	4	5	6	7	8	9	10

"Is It Really Love—Is It You?"

Answer the following questions with "yes" or "no" in the space provided.

_____ 1. Do you have a great number of things you like to do together?

_____ 2. Do you have a feeling of pride when you compare your friend with anyone else you know?

_____ 3. Do you suffer from a feeling of unrest when away from him/her?

_____ 4. Even when you quarrel, do you still enjoy being together?

_____ 5. Have you a strong desire to please him/her, and are you quite glad to give way on your own preferences?

_____ 6. Do you actually want to marry this person?

_____ 7. Does he or she have the qualities you would like to have in your children?

_____ 8. Do your friends and associates admire this person and think he or she would be a good match for you?

_____ 9. Do your parents think you are in love? (They're very discerning about such things.)

_____10. Have you started planning, at least in your mind, what kind of wedding, children, and home you will have?

Dr. David Seamands, Pastor of the Wilmore Methodist Church in Wilmore, Ky. has identified five voices which a believer can listen to for affirmation of his decision-making ability. No one single voice should carry the total weight of choosing a life partner. The first voice is that of scripture itself. The balance that scripture brings to our attempts at choosing a life partner leads us to balance all areas of our life. It is easy to be infatuated with many individuals with whom we come in contact. It is easy also to think that we have fallen head over heels in love with those same individuals. We can be attracted to believers and non-believers alike. Scripture itself helps us to get a perspective on the kind of person the believer is to marry. It clearly states: "Do not be bound together with unbelievers; for what partnership have righteousness and lawlessness or what fellowship has light with darkness?" (II Cor. 6:14, *NASB*). The believer consequently has really no freedom, except to choose a believer as his partner.

The second voice is that "still small voice" which is God's Spirit guiding us from within, that inner feeling that says, "what I am about to do is okay." It is important to remember to check each voice carefully with the others when determining God's will for so important a decision as the choice of a life partner.

The third voice is based upon providential and experiencial circumstances. This voice is heard as we move through courtship and we see more and more often that this may truly be the partner who God has called to be our companion through life, the parent of our child, and the one who will provide for and nurture us for a lifetime.

The fourth voice is often locked in a cell constructed from our own emotions. It has been said that when love comes in, reason flies out the door. We do need to give deep and prayerful consideration to the individual who we may choose, and it is our choice ultimately, for our life partner.

The fifth voice may actually be a chorus of voices. It is the affirmation provided by other individuals who play significant roles in our lives. Whose advice would you seek, and whose counseling would you trust in helping to decide whether it is God's will that you marry an individual or not?

The Wedding

Each of us would like to convey something special on our wedding day. What would you like to say to the witnesses at the time you join another individual and form a new family? In the space provided below, outline the thoughts you would like your wedding to say.

Now, using the thoughts above, write out the vows you would like to share with your mate. What are the commitments you would like to communicate in your wedding ceremony?

NOTES

NOTES